Testimonials and Comments

"Attorney Stuart Furman's uniquely practical workbook is invaluable empowerment for anyone seeking to be properly prepared for the future."

C. Hasz President/CEO
Grace Care Management

"As my characters Earl and Opal have discovered, growing older has its ups and downs. My comics have always been about the funny side of growing older, but the less humorous side of aging can be difficult for families to handle. *The ElderCare Ready Book* is a valuable tool to help families brace for the challenges ahead and get through the difficulties of aging by becoming more organized and prepared."

Brian Crane,
Creator of the Pickles comic strip

"*The ElderCare Ready Book* is a valuable resource for those taking care of an elderly family member. Mr. Furman hit the nail on the head when writing this book. When the caregiver is in the workforce, using The ElderCare Ready Book to be organized and prepared for their caregiving voyage will help reduce productivity loss for the employee, human resources department, and company owners."

Natasha Sandrock Arthur, PHR-CA, CCP, GRP
Director, Human Resources
CaVU Consulting, Inc.
President of San Diego Society for
Human Resource Management (2013–2014)

The ElderCare
READY BOOK

STUART FURMAN

Dedication & Thanks

Dedicated to:

Seymour Furman, my dad;

Marion Furman, my mom;

Miriam Bender, my wife's mother;

Charles Evans, my wife's father; and

Eugene Bender, my mother-in-law's second husband,

all of whom provided the inspiration for this book.

Special thanks to

my wife, Jayne, and

Cara Ouellette, my legal assistant,

for their valuable insight and assistance.

Very special thanks to:

Brian Crane,

creator of the Pickles comic strip,

for his comment and permitted use of his comic strips in this book.

CONTENTS

Pickles by Brian Crane

Why This Book Is So Important

The need for families to assist in the caregiving of the older generation is on the rise, along with its attendant stresses, strains, frustrations, and time commitments.

The cared-for senior also feels uneasiness and guilt, as well as the same frustrations, stresses, and strains due to slowly losing control of independence, affairs, and health.

The common goal here is to bridge the gap between generations so that the aging process can be more comfortable, controllable, and understandable.

As described in this book, family caregiving or eldercare fits into two models. Many families care for their loved ones at their homes and provide assistance with activities of daily living, such as bathing, grooming, toileting, feeding, and the like. Other families have their loved ones living in some sort of facility, whether it be an independent living community, assisted living community, board-and-care home, or even a nursing home.

No matter which model applies, eldercare is the oversight and management of a loved one's personal care (either at home or in a facility), along with other things that need to be taken care of for them, such as handling their finances, driving them to doctor appointments, and more.

Who Will Provide Eldercare?

I have found in my law practice that eldercare situations do not always involve parent–child relationships. Our definition of family has changed. There are many more second or third marriages. There are "yours, mine, and ours" families when referring to children. Many family members care for their stepparent as if he or she were their own. This was the case with my mother-in-law and her second husband after she was widowed. I have seen the younger generations taking care of aunts and uncles, brothers and sisters, and other distant relatives and friends. So for purposes of this book, I refer to the older generations as the "elder" or "elders," but keep in mind that this definition can apply to the above relationships or to others.

Who Is This Book For?

This book is for people who are providing eldercare to an elder and for the elders who are being cared for. It is intended to assist you in helping to care for an elder with their full consent, cooperation, and knowledge. This book is not intended to be a resource for anyone to access another person's information without their consent. Consent must be established either through discussion with that person while they are mentally competent, or via previously established communication and agreement, such as by the elder executing a power of attorney, living trust, or other legal documentation, giving appropriate authority for a person to act on their behalf. Above all, it is vital to protect the well-being of the elder, including their financial and personal privacy, to the greatest extent possible. Ideally, this book and other eldercare publications should be used for you to work together with the elder to prepare for future issues and events. The information in this book should never be used to take advantage of an elderly person, to act on the elder's behalf without authority, or to utilize the elder's information in a way that may compromise his or her personal, financial, and legal privacy and security.

What Is This Book About?

This book is about having, immediately at hand, the organized, complete, and necessary information and documentation to manage your loved one's health and other affairs when the elder is unable to do so on his or her own.

Attorneys draft legal documents that say when the elder is no longer able to care for his or her affairs, they allow another person to take control. But what happens after that? What is the game plan? How do you prepare for this? What do you actually do? What information and documentation is needed to have a seamless transition in the elder's management of his or her affairs?

This book does not ask open-ended questions. It prompts you to collect relevant information and documentation for your eldercare journey and gives you real information about how to make your journey better and easier for both you and the elder.

Although your elder's care needs will continually vary,

this book prepares you for whatever divergence they will take. Countless events can happen, and it is impossible to direct someone as to all the situations that arise. Therefore it is vitally important to be prepared in advance for the decisions that await you. This book is a tool to deal with the foreseeable and unforeseeable events that you will experience on your journey.

This book also contains a glossary of certain terms that you will come across and a description of the types of care provided by independent care providers that you will run into. These resources can only be general descriptions by nature, as each part of the country may use different terms, but the general description for each is the same. Study these terms because you will come across them often.

I hope that the information in this book will help dissipate some of your anxiety through preparation. It did for me.

Chapter 1

INTRODUCTION

MY BACKGROUND IS A PROFESSIONAL violinist turned attorney. I started studying the violin at age nine. I played the violin professionally in symphony and chamber orchestras for several years during my college tenure and through the first few years of my law practice. What I learned from that experience, in addition to the incredible discipline that it took to become a competent musician, was the preparation necessary to give a solid performance. It took hours and hours of practice and rehearsals before each concert. If I was unprepared for the performance, the stress, strain, and fear of standing out with a wrong note or musical error kept me more determined to practice harder for the next concert. As they say, practice makes perfect, and it was a valuable lesson that stayed with me for my entire life.

I began the practice of law in December of 1981 after passing the California State Bar on my first attempt the year prior. Not knowing exactly in what area of law I was going to practice, I opened an office with a law school buddy and took whatever cases came in the door. It was a real eye-opener seeing that the "knowledge" of law that I learned in law school was far different from the "practice" and the "business" of law in the real world. Being prepared for my clients and their legal matters was important to me so I could be the best lawyer that I could be.

After roughly twenty years of having practiced elder law and estate planning, another similarly life-altering experience happened to me. We seemed to have been caught totally off-guard when my wife, Jayne, and I realized one day that our parents, each in their own way, had reached that golden age when their health started to fail, mentally or physically. They were our parents, and that couldn't happen to them. They will never get sick. They will never get old. Jayne's dad passed away from emphysema in 1996 after a lengthy illness. He was mentally competent the whole time, but physically he needed assistance toward the end. Jayne's mom remarried, and her second husband passed away from cancer. He too was mentally competent but also needed physical assistance toward the end. Jayne's mom today at ninety years of age is doing really well, considering two trips to the nursing home in the last five years. Luckily, she is mentally competent and has a great spirit.

My parents are a completely different story. My dad, who is eighty-seven years old, had shown signs of dementia for many years and had a long, steady, and very rough decline. He currently lives in a six-bed board-and-care home, is totally bed bound, and is mentally "out to lunch," as I humorously say to keep me from thinking about the reality of his current life. He was by all accounts a brilliant man, and now he has no serious thoughts or quality of life. My mother, who is eighty-six years old, also has cognitive impairment, can communicate only in the moment, has short-term memory loss, and is on the edge physically.

A parent's decline just sneaks up on you, and denial plays a big part in that. I think that most of my readers will relate to some of the following events. These are just a couple milestone events we experienced. Those who have not yet started their eldercare journey need to know that these events are just a very small fraction of things that occurred along our journey, and we are still traveling on it.

Chapter 2

DECLINE

Pickles by Brian Crane

MY DAD'S DECLINE HAS BEEN the toughest of all of our parents, but there were surprises that we all appreciated. My father was always the dominant member of the family. He was a psychiatrist by trade. He happened to always be right, and no one could prepare well enough to win a debate with him. We started to notice a hint of forgetfulness. Then there was a hint of confusion. These were very subtle changes, and we wrote it off to the aging process. As things progressed, we saw telltale signs of dementia: less grooming and bathing, increased anger, increased frustration with daily life, increased forgetfulness, and so forth. My mother, my wife, and my siblings discussed his decline, and my mom was on board to try assisted living. Dad was the holdout.

Our family finally realized that even with aging, unfortunately there was my dad's likely diagnosis of dementia or Alzheimer's disease. However, it didn't matter what we called it. What was important was how we handled it in the real world. Things got dicey for a while. The first major hurdle was to get my mom and dad to leave their home and move to independent living. One of those surprises that my dad gave us just at the right time was his realization that he was declining mentally, and he was interested in looking at assisted living communities in anticipation of moving later.

Many of the older generations think that living anywhere except in their own residence is living in the dreaded "home." They think of the home as "the nursing home" where most of their parents lived until they died. They don't want their kids to put them in a home, and thus there is more resistance to moving than you would expect. Times have changed, however, and there are many more living options now, from home care to independent living, assisted living, memory care, and board and care, all of which are lower levels of care than the nursing home and allow people to maintain a greater level of independence. Typically, the assisted living facilities are called communities to better reflect the lifestyle to be enjoyed there, including movies in their own movie theaters, activities, live entertainment, happy hours, and more. The challenge is to articulate this shift to the older generation that already has a preconceived notion of what to expect. In my law practice, many children of my clients reported that once their folks toured a community, the fear was abated, and they became more receptive to alternate living quarters.

In my case, once the opportunity presented itself, we immediately started looking at communities primarily to get my folks over the stigma of thinking that they were going to a "home." We toured about five communities and got their feedback. That helped us refine our search later.

Then there was an incident at their residence. My dad called me and said it was probably time to consider assisted living. To this day, we don't know what happened, but thankfully it was nothing serious. My folks just wanted to "try out" the assisted living experience. Hurrah! However, there were two deal-breakers for my dad in making their decision. First, they wanted the option to come back home if they didn't like it. Second, they did not want a long-term lease in the community so that they could come back home. We made a deal that their residence would stay vacant, furnished, and ready for them to come back. We would pick up their mail and make sure the yard was kept up. The only requirement was that my folks had to give it at least a six-month trial. It would be like they were on a six-month vacation. If they didn't like assisted living, they could move home. My dad was good with our agreement, so plans were made. The rest of the family knew that my folks were probably not going to move back home, but the little white lie was necessary to urge them along.

Another incident I remember was when my folks drove to visit their dear friends of fifty years and got lost. That was another one of those events that just shakes you. We then knew the keys to the car had to go, but how could we tell my parents that they could no longer drive? Another surprise for us came along. My dad said he felt he could no longer drive and handed over the keys. Wow! The car was immediately sold to seal his decision. This is not an easy thing for the majority of my clients' families who deal with this issue. We got lucky! The great news was that my folks were no longer driving, protecting themselves and others on the road. The bad news was that they had no transportation, so the family now had to start helping them with doctor visits, trips to the store, and other excursions. The assisted living community to where they moved had a community car and driver, but it was often tough to schedule the times and days that my folks needed. They tested us periodically by needing rides at odd times to see whether, and how quickly, we would come over.

As my dad's decline continued, he became more aggressive. My wife and I were awakened countless times in the middle of the night with my mother calling to say that we need to come over because my dad was "crazy." I could hear him in the background yelling and screaming at her. He was in another world, and we became very concerned about my mother's safety. We constantly asked my mom if she needed to be separated from him. She did end up staying together with my dad, and we did keep a close eye on them both for safety, so everything turned out alright in the end. However, my dad often said he was going to leave and she could not stop him. There was a lot of swearing.

Then another surprise came along at this point in his life. He walked out of their assisted living apartment a couple of times, but luckily never out of the facility. One time we were prepared to drive over, but once he left, he forgot where he was going! So he sat in the hallway until he calmed down and returned to his apartment. Then on another occasion he left the apartment in his skivvies only and sat on the bench by the elevator. He had now forgotten where he lived!

That was when my dad needed to go into memory care. During the moving process, I was stunned as to what had been going on in their apartment for the prior year or two. My mother just didn't want to tell us. My dad truly had lived there as long as he possibly could. My mom was a real trooper, standing by her husband until she just couldn't do it anymore. So they moved to assisted living with a memory care unit, and they were split up for the first time in their lives. This was very difficult for my mom, but that is why we found a community where they both could live, just in different sections. Dad would be allowed out to visit as much as my mom wanted him to. It sounds kind of cruel, but he was not mentally well, and in our minds this was the best that could be arranged. After further decline, my dad was moved to a board-and-care facility, where he is homebound and very seriously demented. It is very sad to see him in this condition, given that he was a Harvard graduate and medical doctor. Now he is reduced to gibberish and an occasional "hi" or "thank-you" when his dinner plate is put in front of him. He stays in bed for twelve to eighteen hours a day.

My mom has a different kind of cognitive impairment. She is "in the moment," but the moment keeps occurring over and over. The family frustration elevates when talking with her sometimes because you have the same conversation repeatedly. But then we catch ourselves and realize it is not her. It is the aging process and the disease.

My mom is still doing well comparatively. We take her on outings to the symphony and out to lunch and dinner, and she enjoys herself. She still knows who we are and has a quality of life. However, she has no concept of money, assets, or health care and is not legally competent to make any of those decisions.

My wife's mother is actually the easiest to assist. She is mentally competent (thankfully!) and is always in a good mood. Even when she fell and broke her hip and had to spend a couple of months in a nursing home to recuperate, her spirits were always high.

Don't for one second think that this stuff happens once or twice and then the problem is solved. New issues come up almost daily and have to be dealt with at that moment. Some decisions need to be made immediately, and others can wait. Were there a lot of good times? Absolutely. We had numerous family dinners at the assisted living communities, went out to dinner, socialized, watched football together like we did as kids, and much more. I am trying to give you, the reader, the flavor of the other side of the story of interacting with parents in their "golden years."

So that's my story. I related it because the decline of my parents occurred over a lengthy time. There was no clear starting point, and the need to help them just evolved. The few events described above occurred over six to eight years, but issues arose almost daily. During that time, we had to continually take over more aspects of their lives to keep things running smoothly, and manage these aspects of their lives.

Chapter 3

SO WHAT EXACTLY IS ELDERCARE?

Pickles by Brian Crane

MY WIFE AND I ARE baby boomers. I have two siblings also caring for my parents, but my wife is an only child, so my mother-in-law is all ours! In our case, the assistance we provide to our parents is not with their activities of daily living, such as bathing, grooming, feeding, and bathroom functions, as those are managed by their home-care company, assisted living community, or board-and-care home. However, other families often do provide that intense care with activities of daily living. We also do the following, among other things:

- Manage their finances and investments, pay their bills, and make their deposits
- Manage their mail
- Buy and deliver groceries and other products to them
- Assist with laundry
- Assist with maintaining the home and yard
- Remind them about numerous doctor appointments that are coming up
- Schedule and take them to doctor appointments (and there are many of these!)
- Juggle visits and phone calls with each of them
- Monitor each of their medicines and their health and safety

- Monitor and supervise their independent caregivers, assisted living care, care in the board-and-care home, and nursing home care
- Regularly talk with their financial advisors, CPAs, or accountant, doctors, and other family members
- Have family meetings to discuss upcoming issues
- Manage their tax return preparations
- Handle and manage emergencies
- Coordinate activities and outings

To whatever extent the above activities are being provided to the elder is what I consider "eldercare."

Chapter 4

WHY IS ADDRESSING ELDERCARE SO IMPORTANT?

NOBODY HAS A DIVINE EXEMPTION from providing eldercare to a loved one. I saw this every day in my law practice when I had to advise and consult with clients and families about estate planning and elder law issues. I felt I was a lawyer, psychologist, economist, and mediator all at the same time. Once I had to take to the streets and do the things that my clients were doing and reporting to me, I saw patterns in what prepared them for the eldercare role ahead of them. The information and documentation needed was the same for everyone, rich or poor and regardless of race or age, marital status, or location. I wrote this book and accompanying handbook to bring my experiences to the table and help other families.

Does eldercare affect our work and personal lives? You bet it does! Most family caregivers are still in the workforce and we love our parents and want to ensure that their lives are as healthy and safe as they can be.

Do our parents want to feel like they are a burden on their family? Definitely not! We don't want them to feel like they are a burden. The problem is that they need assistance but don't want to ask for help. Additionally, they want the family interaction but also realize that the family has their own needs as well.

In the past, the older generations moved in with the

younger generations when they needed more care. The family managed all the above tasks for their elder family member, and the elder had all the interaction with the people they cared about: the family. Other countries still follow this tradition, and the caregiving can be much more structured as there is often a team of family caregivers to help.

In the United States, however, for better or for worse, society has changed. For example, very few parents live with their children. In fact, less than one-third of the parents polled in a Gallup & Robinson survey said they would even live with an adult child when they could no longer live on their own.[1] Children leave the home to become independent when they are able to. The aging parent is also quite cautious about living with an adult child in their older years, no matter how well they get along, and the thought of doing so is quite disconcerting for them.

Additionally, more families will need to supplement the care of their elder for a variety of reasons. Costs of administering the care, such as labor, food, transportation, and housing, are increasing annually. This will price more families out of the market for caregiving by independent companies or caregivers. Medical science is keeping people alive longer but perhaps not with the commensurate mental capacity or physical well-being. The baby boomer population is coming of age and will create a huge burden on available outside care assistance resources, so there may be more demand than supply of caregivers and facilities, which will also increase prices.

---

1   Carol Bradley Bursack, "Do Parents Really Want to Live with Their Adult Children?" www. Agingcare.com, 2014.

So the eldercare role and private lives must be balanced. This balancing, however, has a certain time commitment and cost associated with it. These facts are not intended to bring guilt on the elder for getting old and feeling like a burden. They are just the facts of life. They are what they are! I am a child of my parents. I feel honored to be able to help them in their older years as they assisted me in my childhood, and my parents should not feel like they are a burden! Simply put, the eldercare journey must be approached in an organized and logical manner to minimize any emotional baggage and to make the caregiving system a smoothly running machine.

Chapter 5

WHY DO I CALL THIS AN ELDERCARE JOURNEY?

I HAVE FOUND THAT ELDERCARE has a beginning point (albeit sometimes hard to recognize) and a clear ending point, with many stops along the way. I compare the eldercare journey to taking an extended trip. It is a real excursion, just not in the traditional sense.

If you were going to take a vacation and were not familiar with your travel destination, would you not do some research to find where to stay, what to see, and what the costs would be, make hotel reservations, and determine how you were going to travel from point A to point B? Your general itinerary would be somewhat set, but your real-time experiences would be determined by your interactions with your environment in the moment. You would also pack your suitcase with everything that you need or might need for the entire trip—perhaps your passport, other identification, tickets, credit cards, clothes, shoes, toiletries, and more. You might also bring your bathing suit just in case the weather was nice and there was an opportunity to take a dip. You might also pack that foreign language book in case you wanted to try out the native language. These are things that you may never use but might want or need.

This book is designed to help you pack for your eldercare journey. It provides you guidance as to what you will need, what you may need, or just what would make life easier if you had it on hand. There will be many adventures on your journey, and you will need to be ready for them, not knowing in advance what they might be! Those will be handled in the moment. Like taking the extended vacation where you pack everything that you will need along the way, prepare for your eldercare journey by packing everything that you need, might need along the way, or could use if the situation called for it.

Maybe you have already experienced some of the disorganization (and its attendant stresses and strains) that go hand in hand with eldercare. Perhaps some of you have already completed your eldercare journey, and your parents or other loved one has passed away. If not, I submit that everyone will need to travel on this journey to some degree.

For most family caregivers and the elders, the eldercare journey can feel a bit overwhelming, especially at first. Where do you start? How big a suitcase will I need? Do you even know how to prepare? Do you know what to pack? How long will your journey be? Perhaps the elder is quite self-sufficient right now and has no specific needs. Most people, however, don't want to conceptualize that an illness, injury, or simply normal aging can change these circumstances in a New York minute!

Statistics, numbers, and intangible effects of eldercare can be alarming, especially if you are just beginning your journey. Many people don't realize that preparing can eliminate much of the uncertainty that can accompany eldercare responsibilities. You and your family, especially your loved one, can take steps now that will help you prepare for your eldercare journey.

The elders in your life are right now the most mentally competent and healthy that they will be. Take advantage of that to assist you in your preparation to identify and locate what you will need to set in motion the shift in management.

The eldercare role is not something to be feared or avoided because, like death and taxes, it will occur.

Don't fear it. Just be prepared for it.

Knowledge, organization, and preparation are empowering and comforting.

For the elder, this organization and preparation brings solace in knowing that he or she won't have to worry as much about future care or money.

Chapter 6

WHEN IS THE RIGHT TIME TO START YOUR ELDERCARE JOURNEY?

Pickles by Brian Crane

WHAT IF A FIRE WAS closing in on your home, and you were ordered to immediately evacuate? I live in a remote area in Southern California, and it has happened to me more than once. Have you decided what you will take from your home when filling your valuable car space? I must confess that I had not planned for this the first time I had to evacuate, but I realized it was extremely important and prepared well for the next time. If you have not adequately prepared, it is likely that you will not make the best decision under the pressure and strain of the evacuation.

Your loved one will experience issues that you will need to quickly deal with, many of which cannot be anticipated. Delay has real consequences by forcing immediate decisions without adequate information at hand, which in turn could adversely affect your loved one's health and care.

Preparation provides knowledge, power, and most importantly the comfort of knowing that you are ready for the eldercare challenge.

There is an old joke that you do not have Alzheimer's disease if you just can't find your keys, but you may have it if you can't remember what the keys are for! Look for the signs that changes are occurring with your elder. You are the best judge of changes in his or her life as you can detect very small nuances in his or her behavior and/or mental status.

This may mean that the fire is simmering. Consider the following examples:

- Changes in gait or walk; difficulty bending over
- Weight loss
- Repeated falls or mysterious bruises
- Neglected personal hygiene (bathing, grooming, brushing teeth, wearing same clothes daily, difficulty dressing)
- Incontinence
- Difficulty eating
- Lack of cooking or shopping; lack of food in the house or spoiled food
- Unmaintained or uncleaned house and/or yard
- Change in mental attitude
- Lack of calls to family
- Problems with bills (bills not being paid or being paid twice; mail not being opened)
- Credit card debt increasing
- Unusual or mysterious checks to individuals or charities
- Inconsistent spending, increased donations, or new subscriptions
- Driving problems, such as tickets or dents in car
- A new, young best friend
- Hoarding
- Nonemergency calls to you in the middle of the night
- Increasingly short temper
- Forgetfulness

- Tendency to get lost, even in his or her neighborhood
- More argumentative

The list is endless, so keep your eyes and ears open when you are with the elder for subtle signs. Be careful not to deny that they exist.

Very important: If your elder is losing mental competency, it is critical to take immediate action to gather all your elder's information and documentation and to ensure that you have the authority in place to manage the elder's affairs. The elder is the treasure trove of the information that you will need as you travel forward. You must access that information while he or she is able to accurately communicate it to you.

Do you think that you are already well prepared?

I thought that I was, but I was constantly presented with situations that needed information that I did not have with me. Because our first home evacuation was disorganized and traumatic, my wife and I then planned well for the next event. Likewise, we remembered this for our next eldercare event, and planned accordingly. You might think that you are very well prepared, but I suspect you have not thought about many of the items in this book. Believe it or not, when I completed my collection of just necessary information, it exceeded a hundred pages!

Have you also thought about your loved one's eldercare needs if something happened to you? Is your spouse also prepared to take over? Your kids? Will the elder's family caregiving have a seamless transition? The second time my wife and I had to evacuate our home, I was out seeing a client.

The fire department did not let me back into the neighborhood to assist her in the evacuation. But she was also ready due to our detailed preparation where we selected the items that needed to go. Simply put, our plan was predetermined, so the second evacuation was much less stressful.

Along your eldercare journey, be alert! Ask questions. I tell my clients all the time that there is no such thing as a stupid question. Demand answers. Don't be bashful. Your loved one's health and possibly life is at stake! Decisions that you will have to make need to make sense to you, so don't just rely on what is being told to you as being the best course for your elder. Make sure you have a complete picture of options. Tragically, I found that many health care professionals in a variety of positions withheld options from me to further a policy agenda. Use the Internet religiously but be cognizant that what you read on the Internet may not always be accurate.

Most important, keep your information and documentation always at hand. The information is no good to you if you don't have it when you need it. You will always need it with routine tasks, and a crisis always happens at the most inopportune time. This is why I advise my clients against putting estate planning documents in a safe deposit box. Loved ones always have a habit of needing a hospital trip between Friday evening and Sunday evening. Guess what? Banks are not open, so you cannot access the documents, especially the health care directive or HIPAA release, so these documents become worthless for that crisis event.

Are you ElderCare Ready? If not, then read on.

Chapter 7

CONTINUING THE JOURNEY

I WROTE THIS BOOK BASED on my own eldercare journey, which continues as of the printing of this book. When I first started my eldercare journey, I was terribly unprepared, even though I was an elder law attorney. What happens in real life is very different from what you may think is supposed to happen. The goal of this book is to help you become more organized and prepared, giving you and your family peace of mind so that you are empowered and ready for the eldercare journey. Organization and preparation reduces time spent, money expended, and anxiety experienced. I can't eliminate your journey, but I can assist you in collecting the information and documentation that you will need. Do it now.

This book suggests that you collect and have available voluminous amounts of information and documentation. If you will need all this information and documentation depends on your elders and the challenges that they present. The more information and documentation you have collected and the more you have taken the suggested actions described in this book, the more prepared and effective you will be when you need it. You, your family, and your elder will experience fewer delays and less stress.

This book will always be a work in progress. Health care laws and rules change, new illnesses are constantly being discovered, new protocols in the delivery of health care are being implemented, new medicines are discovered to help seniors live longer, new information and/or documentation may need to be included in this book, different states deal with issues differently, and new techniques to handle elder-care challenges are being discovered. Don't limit your collection of information and/or documentation only to what is included herein. Every eldercare journey is different.

Finally, how did I simplify the process? From my personal experiences, I created an eldercare system in a fill-in-the-blanks format to prompt me to fill in the information and documentation that I needed, still need, and may need in the future. These prompts are not just open-ended questions but are specifically designed to elicit the exact information needed. Unbelievably, this handbook has now exceeded a hundred pages, and took hundreds of hours to complete! If you don't want to reinvent the wheel, this handbook system is called the *ElderCare Ready Pack* and is available by going to my website at www.eldercareready.com.

The bottom line is that it's never too early to prepare! I surmise that since you are reading this book, it is time.

Start packing!

Chapter 8

INFORMATION AND DOCUMENTATION FOR YOUR ELDERCARE JOURNEY SUITCASE

ON MY OWN ELDERCARE JOURNEY, I have found the information and documentation that was needed, so far, can be divided into ten manageable categories:

(1) Personal Information
(2) Contacts
(3) Medical information
(4) Current living situation
(5) Desired facilities
(6) Pets
(7) Financial
(8) Estate plan
(9) Service providers
(10) Miscellaneous

The importance of collecting this information cannot be overstated. You will need information when you have to act for your elder. Collect this information NOW when there is no crisis at hand and while your elder is as mentally competent as possible to assist you. This process is a joint effort, and although the below information is voluminous, once it is completed, you will have your suitcase packed and be ready to travel on your eldercare journey.

Please be aware that none of the following discussion relieves the necessity to have "releases" on file with each individual or company for which you are accessing information. Releases are explained in detail in the next chapter. You need the below information *and* to have releases on file to access the information and documentation. Remember that information, such as an account balance, changes all the time, so you will need to access accounts and data more than once.

Also, don't forget that the elder may not be in a position to answer any questions when needed; thus you need to collect all the appropriate information and documentation on their behalf.

(1) Personal Information

Personal Information about the elder is vital to access accounts, medical records, and other information needed to manage the care of your elder. For example, information such as mother's maiden name is often important to satisfy security questions when accessing bank accounts. The elder's spouse's name, prior spouse's name, social security number, place of birth, and date of birth are often additional security questions. Since you do not know which one will be asked, you need to collect them all. You may have recently also noticed a requirement to lodge answers to very personal questions, such as the name of the person's first high school or the name of the individual's first pet. These need to be written down and kept available at all times.

A complete physical description of the elder is important in case someone is trying to find your elder, who may have wandered off due to dementia or has simply gotten lost. A picture would be important to have, perhaps on your smart-phone, for identification purposes.

Many elders have implants or other devices, such as pacemakers, knee or shoulder replacements, heart stents, or prosthetics. Detailed information for each device is needed to assist medical providers who transport a patient or before a person undergoes a medical procedure. Complete descriptions for the devices, including model numbers and serial numbers, need to be acquired. Some of these devices may have been in place for many years, and doctors can change or records may be lost or difficult to locate, so you cannot always rely on your doctor to have this information readily available.

Other medical devices need to be listed. These include dentures, hearing aids, walkers, catheters, glasses, braces, and any other specific devices for your elder. In assisted living communities for example, if these items are lost (or sometimes stolen, I must unfortunately admit); replacements can be easily ordered if the detailed information is readily at hand. Insurance policies can also replace these items when a detailed description is provided.

Any physical limitations that the elder may have are important to list. Is your elder ambulatory and able to walk? Is he or she incontinent? Deaf? Need assistance with other activities of daily living such as bathing, eating, walking, and the like? By listing these limitations, others who assist your elder can be immediately brought up to speed on the elder's physical condition and limitations.

(2) Contact Information

Collect full contact information for the elder's family and friends. Unfortunately, not all families get along with each other. In fact, in my experience dealing with thousands of families over the years, getting along is rare. So you will need to collect and have on hand the key members of your elder's friends and family with detailed contact information. In emergencies or an end-of-life crisis, there is no time to determine who should be contacted and how to contact them.

This list must identify who will act on behalf of the elder as his or her agent or trustee and in which order they will act. The type of document under which the agent or trustee has authority should also be identified, whether a financial power of attorney, living trust, health care directive or power of attorney, or other document. Whether the authority granted is currently effective or needs to have action taken to spring the authority is also important (see chapter nine for more information).

Having all names and contact information for professionals who work with the elder is imperative for quick contact when needed. These professional contacts need to be listed with detailed contact information. You need to confirm that a release is on file with each one of them to be able to communicate with them on behalf of the elder (in chapter nine). Keep in mind that most elders have many more doctors than you realize, so include them all. Again, emergencies happen at the most inopportune times, so you always need to be ready for whatever is thrown at you, when it is thrown at you. Consider dentists, pharmacists, podiatrists, geriatric care managers, physical therapists, and others in the loop for treating your elder when compiling this list.

Legal and financial contacts are equally important. Complete contact information for the elder's attorney, financial planner, accountant, conservator or guardian, and insurance agents for homeowners, renters, long-term care, disability, auto, burial, life, and annuities needs to be collected.

Complete contact information for the funeral home or mortuary should be collected. Contacts for religious services need to be obtained, and your elder needs to tell you whether predeath services are desired. If your elder wants a funeral, whom are you inviting? What type of service? Only the elders know who is important to them. Get the list!

(3) Medical Information

Health insurance and coverage information is needed each time your elder goes to the doctor or hospital. Always have this information ready, and make sure you have copies of the health insurance card(s) and prescription drug card(s) with you.

Updated and current medical information is critical for managing the elder's care. Medical conditions need to be listed and reviewed continually because trips to the doctor or hospital may not be to your elder's regular physician, meaning that medications can be missed or overlooked. HMOs (a type of insurance policy provider network) are notorious for having rotations of treating physicians so the medical record needs to be accurate because the doctor relies on it when treating the elder.

The recurring and nonrecurring medication lists are of utmost importance. A recurring medication is one taken on a regular basis to manage a specific illness or condition. For example, a statin drug used to manage high cholesterol that is taken every evening is a recurring medication. However, an antibiotic taken on a periodic or temporary basis for a urinary tract infection would be a nonrecurring medication.

In my eldercare journey, I have found that drugs may be prescribed for a particular condition, but then it is discovered later that they were not terminated when they should have been. This happened in our case numerous times due to poor communication between the assisted living facility and the physician's office. The elder's medications (both recurring and nonrecurring) should be reviewed often, and you should contact the doctors if you believe that a medication should be eliminated. This is a strange statement, but *don't ever rely on the medical community knowing what medication the elder is taking.*

Since the medications and dosages that the elder actually take will be quite lengthy and will change often, you should create a "short list" of the medications that does not include the comprehensive medicine description. For example, if your elder goes to the hospital, they will want to know the drug, dosage, and frequency. This is the quick list. However, in other circumstances, you will need to know the prescription numbers, the prescribing doctor(s), the pharmacy, and other identifying information, especially when reordering. This should be kept on a comprehensive list.

(4) Current Living Situation

You need complete information on where your elder is currently living. For example, if your elder lives in an assisted living community, you should list the facility name, address, telephone, fax number, e-mail address, and direct numbers for the executive director, nurse, activities director, billing officer, and any other person in a position of authority. This information will be needed numerous times on your eldercare journey.

Considering that the information may be accessed by someone other than you, you need complete contact information for the elder even if the elder lives at his or her home, including address, telephone numbers, fax number (if any), and an e-mail address.

If he or she lives at a facility, such as assisted living, you need to list all the services currently being provided, such as medicine management, bathing, grooming, toileting, feeding, and others.

You need to list the payment source for the facility—such as veterans benefits, long-term care insurance, private pay, Medi-Cal, or Medicaid—and the monthly cost for the facility. Have the billing person's name and contact information readily at hand. There are always errors in the monthly bills! Watch the bill for services that were never provided. The assisted living community where my mother-in-law lives provides shower assistance. Occasionally, the shower assistant does not show up, but the billing department does not know this. So the bill needs to be scrutinized each month for proper billing. You need to talk with the elder to confirm that the services are actually being provided.

(5) Desired Facilities

Simply put, if the elder has a health issue, where do you want him or her to go for treatment or to live? This sounds simple, and you may think it can be done when the need arises. Trust me, do this research now, when there is no crisis at hand, to give you the time to properly select the appropriate facility and/or care situation for your elder. You need to select a facility or care type in each care category, as you never know what crisis will occur, when it will occur, or the extent of the treatment needed. The most common care facility or care type categories are home care, home health, independent living, assisted living, board and care, memory care, nursing home, rehabilitation center, and hospital. If possible, take the elder along when researching and touring facilities. The elder is the one that will be living there, and the last thing you want is for the elder to say, "I don't like it here," *after* he or she has moved in!

My wife and I remember receiving one of those dreaded telephone calls in the middle of the night from my mother-in-law's assisted living home (any call in the middle of the night is never good!) because she had fallen. Of course, she was going to be taken to the hospital. We immediately directed them to make sure that the first responders took her to the hospital that we selected. There was no time to research this or to preview the hospital in advance. Had we not determined the hospital in advance, she would have been transported to what we would call an inferior care center. We also let the assisted living community know this choice up front in case we were not available when the emergency occurred.

Additionally, once my mother in law could be discharged to a facility, the discharge planner at the hospital asked which nursing home we would like her to be transported to for rehabilitation. The discharge planner presented us with a list of locations to choose from. Instead of having to use the "eenie meenie miney mo" method, we were prepared and directed that she be discharged to our preferred facility. Unfortunately, once your elder is admitted to a specific nursing home, it is very difficult to get the person transferred. In my opinion, I would not want my worst enemy to live in some of these places. The bottom line is that you need to find the desired facility prior to the need.

Assisted living homes are no different. There are numerous considerations in selecting an assisted living home, such as proximity to family, hospitals, doctors, and others; the operator; the cleanliness of the home; the price; and much more. Senior referral agencies may be able to assist as long as you understand that they are paid a commission from the facility that admits your elder, and sometimes their motivation may be to have the elder move into the most expensive home to maximize their commissions. Additionally, compatible homes may not be referred to you if the home does not have a contract with that particular referral agency, thus limiting your choices.

This is an area where the control of your elder's health care can be shifted back to you! I cannot stress more the importance of doing this research in advance. Find the hospital, nursing home, rehabilitation center, assisted living facility, board-and-care facility, or home-care company that you want for your elder and create a full contact list for each of them.

The tendency is to procrastinate in this area, as there is no current need. Do it now. Then you must relate this information to the front-line people who will direct the first responders and third parties managing your elder's care.

Emergency housing is an important consideration for temporary environmental crises. I live in San Diego County, which can be a tinderbox if there is less than normal rainfall during the year. Recently, we had eight wildfires flaming at the same time.

Getting a call to evacuate yourself is one thing, but getting a call to evacuate your mother in assisted living is another. You will have medicines, diapers, food, clothes, walkers, and their own panic to deal with. What if more than one elder is in an assisted living facility? This will only add to the chaos and confusion during an emergency. Plan for this if you are in an area prone to natural disasters. You need to determine where they will go in an emergency and list all contact information. Communicate this to the community or facility where the elder is living so that if you are not available to assist in the transport, they know where to take your elder.

(6) Pets

Pets are the forgotten loved ones! Where will they go if their owners are institutionalized? Where will they go if their owners pass away? Who will take care of them on a temporary basis if the owner is in the hospital? What are their medications and medical needs? Their care must not be forgotten.

Make a full list of answers for the above questions. Additionally, you need to have the veterinarian's contact information and emergency ER for the pet(s) determined and located.

(7) Financial Information

Preparing a complete financial picture of your elder's estate is important when making any financial decisions. You cannot have a suitcase of bank statements, investment statements, deeds, leases, and other documentation with you at all times, so you at least have the information readily at hand with releases on file.

Real Property

It is important to have data on the elder's real estate, including the type of property (single-family residence, condominium, co-op, time share, mobile home, raw land, etc.), the value, and assessor parcel numbers. Many properties have outstanding mortgages or loans. It is important to know the lender and payment information. Other information is also important, such as homeowners' insurance policy details, homeowner association (HOA) payment amounts, and to whom the HOA payment is due. Additionally, keep a record of tenant information if the property is rented. It is also important to know the current vesting (the exact legal ownership information) of the property. You need to know if automatic payments are in place for any outstanding loans, property tax bills, or other payments and from which accounts they are paid.

Financial Accounts

For bank accounts, you will need information about each account. This will include the bank, information about which branch the elder usually uses, account number, and the exact title of the name on the account. It is also important to keep information about automatic deposits and from whom they come, as well as automatic payments (including from which account they are paid and to whom). Keeping track of automatic transactions is important to make sure that bills are paid on time and that automatic deposits are received when they are due. The address where statements are mailed, who can sign on the account, debit card numbers, PIN numbers, and online banking information, including passwords and usernames is also important information that you will need.

As to brokerage accounts, similar information is needed, including whether the accounts are qualified (IRA, 401(k) or other retirement account) or nonqualified (all other accounts). Like with bank accounts, keep the following information available: brokerage company name, branch, account number, name on the account, value in the account, whether there are automatic payments, to whom and from which account the automatic payments are sent, deposits and where the deposits are coming from, where statements are mailed, who can sign on the account, debit cards, PIN numbers, and online access information including passwords and usernames.

Annuities have slightly different requirements. For these, collect the insurance company name, annuitant, and whether the annuity is a qualified or a nonqualified annuity. It is also recommended to note the cash value in the annuity, beneficiary name, and online access information, including passwords and usernames, if online access is available.

For life insurance policies, you need to collect the company contact information, policy number, the name of the insured person, and the beneficiary or beneficiaries. The value and cash value, type of policy (term or a whole life policy with face value), where statements are mailed, PIN numbers, and online access information including passwords and usernames is also valuable information to have at hand.

Cars and Other Vehicles

List the year and make, license plate number, name on title, lender with contact information, loan number and balance, and the location of the vehicle, the keys, and the pink slip. Keep the same information handy for the fancy toys like motorhomes, boats, airplanes, and other exotic vehicles.

Debts and Income

Your elder's creditors must be identified to ensure prompt and correct payment. Collect the creditor name and address, account numbers, where the statements are mailed, type of debt (credit card, line of credit, auto loan, personal note, or other), balance owed, average balance, regular payment amount and due date, and current interest rate. Credit card fraud is unfortunately very common and having this information available will help you to keep track of credit and debts for the elder. Also, keep track of whether there is an automatic payment from the elder's account and from which account the payment is taken.

The elder's income and sources of income must be identified. This includes social security and to whom it is paid (the elder, the spouse, or both), pension source information, IRAs or other retirement accounts, rental income, and other investment income.

Other Valuables

Is there a home safe? List the location in the residence, who has access to it, and the location of the key or combination, and the current contents.

Is there a safe deposit box? If so, determine the location with all contact information for the bank branch, the box number, and who has access to the box and the contents. CAUTION: if you are not a signatory on the safe deposit box, you will most likely not be able to access the box, even with a power of attorney or living trust.

All the above information may be needed even when you are merely reviewing the elder's transaction history, assisting the elder, or have taken control over the elder's finances. Additionally, you must know the location of the appropriate documentation relative to each category.

(8) Estate Planning Documents

Having copies of estate planning documents is critical as they are often requested by financial institutions and heath care providers so they know who is in charge, if the documents have not been previously submitted to them. Decisions can then be made quickly. Additionally, all professionals and service providers should have the appropriate legal documents, including a release, power of attorney, or living trust, approved and on file before a crisis. The documents may need to be reviewed by a provider's legal counsel and in a crisis situation time is of the essence.

You should also list the critical information about the elder's estate plan, including the name or title of his or her living trust, the trustees with contact information for each, the dates of the trust and amendments thereto, and the location of the documents for each trust.

You need the same information relative to the elder's last will and testament, durable power of attorney, health care advance directive, and HIPAA release.

Every estate plan is different, and every attorney has a different way of drafting estate documents. It may be wise to make sure that you fully understand how the elder's estate plan is set up and what your role is, if any, in the estate and legal documents. It is much harder to find out what your duties and options are when in a crisis, so make sure you are clear about how the elder's legal plan works before a crisis occurs.

(9) Service Providers

Collecting this information will save you frustration and time. How many times have you tried to take action for someone and a representative won't talk to you because you are not authorized? Well, get authorized when there is no crisis. Believe me when I say that if the TV goes out, it is a crisis! The phone line going out is a crisis! Know whom to contact with the proper security information, and get yourself on the approved list before there is a problem that you have to address. Releases are explained in more detail in the next chapter.

Which Service Providers Are Important?

Collect telephone and television company information, including the type of account (home, cell, fax), the contact information, account number, customer service number, and any online access passwords and usernames. Internet service provider information should also be available, including the company contact information, account number, online access username and password, and Wi-Fi network name and security or access code.

Collect similar information for other utilities, such as electric, gas or propane, water, and home security system companies, as appropriate.

Is there an identity theft protection service? If so, you need the company name, account number, phone, and online access information. This could be very important if you are acting for the elder as it may cause an identity theft alert if the elder has subscribed to identity theft protection services.

Are there any storage facilities? You need the name of the facility, address, unit numbers, location of key or lock combination, contents of the unit, and the payment amount (to whom paid and when paid).

Transportation providers need to be identified now because it is difficult to arrange for transportation for your elder when there is a medical emergency. Having this arranged ahead of time reduces stress and delays. Who will be the medical transport company, and who will be the nonmedical transport company? List all contact information and determine the pricing structure. Have an account established so you can just order the transport and be billed for the service automatically. In addition, is there a bus or shuttle that the elder will generally take to go places? Which taxis service the elder's area of residence and what is the usual cost?

(10) Miscellaneous

Believe it or not, there will be much more that I didn't even think of, and you need to list and determine if it is important when you realize what it is.

Conclusion

Does this seem extreme or like overkill? I can say that we needed most of the information above at some point along our journey, and our journey is far from complete. Collect this information when there is no crisis. Failure to do so will cost time, money, stress, and a lot of frustration for both you and your loved one.

As I mentioned earlier, you can simplify this process and not reinvent the wheel by visiting my website at www.eldercareready.com. My *ElderCare Ready Pack* contains over a hundred pages of detailed outlines prompting you as to what information you will need. The fill-in-the–blanks format is systematized and will ensure you don't miss important information along your journey.

Happy travels!

Chapter 9

RELEASES

ONE OF THE MOST FRUSTRATING parts of managing the care of an elder is not having access to necessary information when you need it. Again, how many times have you called a company, such as a bank or brokerage company, or a professional, like an attorney or doctor, or anyone else on behalf of another person, and the response is "I cannot give you any information because you are not authorized," or "you are not on the account, so I cannot give you any information"? You need access to information. Knowledge is the key to the eldercare lockbox.

This is an ongoing and evolving problem. Although this chapter is a bit complex, I hope that the following discussion will help alleviate some of your confusion, not increase it, and provide some guidance about how to gain access to your elder's financial, personal, and medical information when needed. If you become frustrated, remember that although it may not give you much comfort, you are certainly not alone!

Throughout this book, you may have seen references to having a "release." I am using this as a very general term, which is intended to mean that the appropriate and necessary document required by the individual or institution (as outlined in this chapter) has been provided and accepted as sufficient to gain access to the elder's information and documentation.

What Is Access Exactly?

Access to information is different from having the ability to sign on the accounts and transact business. Often you may just want information about a bank account balance, a check that cleared, or a credit card charge, but are not looking to sign for the elder or make a transaction. The document required to gain access to the information can often be different from the document needed to have the ability to sign on an account, and a power of attorney is not always better than a release or consent to release information. Unfortunately, institutions (banks, brokerage firms, credit card companies, service companies, etc.) and professionals (doctors, lawyers, accountants, etc.) each have their own rules and policies.

Keep in mind that a power of attorney is signed to give someone the power and authority to act for the person creating the power of attorney, and the authority to have access to information. The sole purpose of a release is to give someone access to information and documentation but not to take action on behalf of the person signing the release.

Ownership Type and Living Trusts

Gaining access to the elder's individually held asset information (such as bank transaction history or account balance history) is accomplished quite differently than gaining access to asset information where the asset is held in a living trust. Simply put, a power of attorney generally has no relevance when asking someone to give information about an asset held in a living trust. It is like comparing apples to oranges. So if you go to the bank with a power of attorney and ask for a balance for an account held in a living trust, the bank will refuse your request.

Generally, access to financial information in a revocable living trust requires a release signed by the trustee (who is typically the elder) in his or her capacity as trustee of the trust. The release has to say something like this: *"I, Jim Roe, trustee of the Jim Roe Living Trust, hereby consent to the release of any and all information…"* If the trustee is not the elder but is another person acting as trustee for the elder's living trust, the acting trustee would issue the release. So the release would say something like this: *"I, Jane Doe, trustee of the Jim Roe Living Trust, hereby consent to the release of any and all information…"* Again, a power of attorney is generally inadequate in this situation, as the elder executed the power of attorney in his or her individual capacity rather than in his or her capacity as trustee. The account held in the trust is not the same as the account of the individual. This gets a bit confusing, but here is an example to help clarify this.

John Smith is a customer at ABC Bank. John has three accounts with ABC Bank:

Account 1: A checking account that the bank shows is owned by John Smith.

Account 2: A checking account that the bank shows is owned by John Smith, trustee of the John Smith Living Trust.

Account 3: An individual retirement account (IRA) that the bank shows is owned by John Smith.

If John's daughter Nancy (for example) wanted to have access to and make transactions on John's accounts, what sort of document might she use to accomplish this?

Account 1: This account is owned by John alone. No other person is listed as an owner on the account. Nancy would use a power of attorney to access the account, if John's power of attorney lists her as the agent who can act on his behalf and the power of attorney gives Nancy the requisite authority to do banking for John.

Account 2: This account is not owned by John individually, even though it is owned by John's own living trust. Therefore, Nancy would not be able to use a power of attorney to access this account. Nancy would need the authority (through a legal document) to be able to act for John's trust. If John is still competent to sign documents, this may be accomplished by amending the John Smith Living Trust and adding Nancy as cotrustee. If John was not competent to sign documents and if she were listed as a successor trustee to John, a showing of John's incompetency perhaps by medical certifications of incapacity will legally secure her as the acting trustee of John's trust. She then has access to the accounts in John's living trust.

Account 3: Like account 1, account 3 is owned by John

Smith individually (not in a trust), so Nancy might be able to use the power of attorney to transact on this account.

Remember that each state has different laws regarding legal documents and each bank, institution, or other entity may have their own rules regarding accessing account information and making transactions, so the above examples may not hold true in every situation.

Also, joint tenancy (such as an account that has two people as account holders), IRA, and 401(k) assets, for example, are not assets of a living trust. Some assets like life insurance may be in the living trust. So it is important to determine how ownership of each of the assets is held to provide the proper releases.

Powers of Attorney (POA)

Some of this is counterintuitive and confusing. This section will also clearly point out why to not just download a power of attorney off the Internet or buy one from the local office supply store. Contrary to folklore, powers of attorney are not all the same and must be reviewed very carefully. Only an attorney should prepare a power of attorney for the elder after consultation as to the type of power of attorney that best fits the elder's personal circumstances.

If a power of attorney is being presented to access the elder's information, make sure that the power of attorney is currently effective. That sounds weird doesn't it? Why sign a power of attorney that is not effective? Determining the type of power of attorney will affect how you access the necessary information and how and when you can act for the elder.

A currently effective power of attorney (POA) is where a person (the "principal") gives another person (the "agent" or "attorney-in-fact") the power to act for the principal. A power of attorney without durable provisions, described below, will terminate upon death or incompetency (legal incapacity) of the principal.

A currently effective durable power of attorney (DPOA) states that the principal is currently granting the authority to the agent (the person who is named to take action for the grantor of the power of attorney). The authority stays in effect after the principal (the one granting the power of attorney) has become legally incapacitated. This is called "durable" language, and without it, as described above, the power of attorney will terminate upon the legal incapacity of the elder. Please see the chapter called Famous Last Words relating to powers of attorney.

Another widely used type of power of attorney is a springing durable power of attorney (SDPOA). This refers to a durable power of attorney that becomes effective only after the principal (the one granting the power of attorney) has become legally incapacitated (this is also durable language). The power of attorney "springs" into effect upon legal incapacity. Many clients only want the power of attorney to be used if they have become incompetent. They may not want to give up control until it is necessary, so this type of POA fits their purposes. Additionally, the definition of incapacity (as used in each particular power of attorney) will be defined within the power of attorney document itself. For example, the springing power of attorney might state that two medical doctors have to certify that the principal is incapacitated in order for the authority under the power of attorney to spring into effect. You cannot use this type of power of attorney until the power has "sprung." It is like a power of attorney in waiting.

You must also look to the authority granted in the POA, DPOA, or SDPOA. Powers of attorney that do not grant all authority to the agent are called limited or special powers of attorney. You may not have been granted the particular authority that you are trying to act upon or use, so the appropriate authority needs to be identified in the document. Additionally, even if the POA, DPOA, or SDPOA states that it gives all possible powers that the principal has to the agent, there are still powers that may not be granted as they are controlled by state statute and must be expressly stated in the document. For example, California law says that the power to gift the principal's assets or to create a trust on behalf of the principal must be specifically drafted ("expressly stated," in legal terms) in the document or it still does not exist.[2] Again, this is even if the power of attorney states that the agent is granted all conceivable authority, whether listed or not listed.

A frustrating aspect of gaining access to information or using powers of attorney is aging, regardless of the type of power of attorney being presented. Many financial institutions will not accept a power of attorney if it is too old, even though by definition in California law, for example, it is still valid and in full force and effect![3] "Too old" is defined by

---

2   Per California Probate Code § 4264.
3   Per California Probate Code § 4127.

the policies of each institution. I have had clients where the company refused to accept a power of attorney that was only six months old, so be sure to check with the institution beforehand. You can easily see a real conundrum when the elder has a "springing" durable power of attorney (one that comes into effect when the elder is no longer competent), and when the elder is later deemed to be legally incapacitated and thus can no longer execute legal documents, the bank says the power of attorney is too old!

Also, many institutions, especially banks, often do not accept powers of attorney other than on their own forms, so you may need to get pushy with the institution to accept the power of attorney that you submit. This has been a frustration for attorneys and families across the country.

Medical Information

Medical records and information are usually accessed using a HIPAA release which is a release of medical information, similar to how a financial release works. This document is signed by the elder, granting a release of medical records and information to the named individuals. Be careful, as a HIPAA form signed at the elder's physician's office may not name you as an authorized party, and you may think you have a valid HIPAA release giving you access to the elder's medical records when you actually do not.

A power of attorney for health care, often called an "advance medical directive" or similar document in your state, may also provide access to medical information but is typically designed to grant you authority to make decisions for the elder if the elder cannot make such decisions on his or her own.

Legal/Attorney Matters

Attorneys will need a release of some sort before disclosing a client's information to any third party. There is a privileged relationship between the elder and his or her attorney (other such relationships exist between doctors and patients and with the clergy, for example). So the confidentiality must be released, or waived, in writing, before the attorney will disclose any information, whether orally or in writing. The release could be signed by an agent under the elder's power of attorney if the power or attorney grants the agent the authority to do so.

Other Professionals

CPAs, financial planners, and other professionals do not enjoy the same legally privileged relationships but often will require a release or consent to allow their information to be disseminated to another person. Similarly, a power of attorney may also be sufficient.

Banks and Financial Institutions

Financial account information held in the elder's name only will generally require a power of attorney or consent to release information to gain access to the financial data.

Safe deposit boxes will generally require your name on the signature card to gain access. Banks often will not accept any type of power of attorney to access the box of the elder.

They also do not know what is in the box, so access is the only way to discover what is in there.

Premade Forms and Releases

Forms downloaded from the Internet may not provide the authority that you need in all situations that you will come across. Tragically, in these cases, you may not be able to have new documents signed by the elder due to his or her incapacity when you are informed that the submitted document is insufficient. If a person is determined to be legally incapacitated (such as when their doctor certifies that they do not have the mental capacity to understand the nature of their personal matters), he or she will no longer be able to sign legal documents (such as a power of attorney, living trust, or last will). In my practice, I have found the Internet documents woefully inadequate in the vast majority of cases. I strongly recommend having an estate planning attorney draft appropriate documents for the elder's particular situation.

What to Do

To ensure that the proper releases or consents are delivered to all the people and companies holding information or documents that you may need along your eldercare journey, contact each one and ask what documents they will accept to grant access. Then, deliver that document to them and confirm that it is effective to grant you access to information, now and in the future. If you are seeking to change the signing authority on an account or asset or to add yourself as a signer, take the same action and ensure that you will be able to transact all necessary business on behalf of your elder when the time comes for you to step in and assist.

If the elder does not yet want you to be able to sign on his or her account, and if the elder is mentally competent, have the power of attorney, living trust, and other estate planning documents reviewed by an estate planning attorney so when the elder is no longer legally competent, you can access the information needed and transact business for the elder. This way, if the document is insufficient for your needs, the elder can execute a replacement document while he or she is still competent to do so.

Chapter 10

FAMOUS LAST WORDS

THIS WAS ONE OF MY favorite chapters to write. Throughout my career as an attorney, I have heard and seen quite a bit. Unfortunately, the following have hit the list of top statements that I have heard from clients. I call them "famous last words." Those who relied on certain misplaced beliefs or understandings, whether innocently or due to belligerence, often ended up costing their family enormous amounts of money and stress.

1. "I just got certifications from my dad's doctor to state that he is not competent so I can have you do a power of attorney and living trust for him."

This is a biggie! For some reason, people do not grasp the concept that one needs to be competent to execute legal documents. I understand that people generally look at what they need to get accomplished first—for example, accessing a bank account because Dad is not able to any more. However, at some point, they are told, informed, or just believe that Dad must not have legal capacity before signing a power of attorney or living trust. This is just backward! Once Dad lacks legal capacity, he can no longer sign any legal documents, including a power of attorney or living trust, intended to be used when Dad became incompetent.

The only recourse is a conservatorship or guardianship proceeding through the court, which is a very costly and time-
consuming process.

2. "Remember that trust and power of attorney that we discussed for my husband last year? Now I need it."

This issue is related to the first one above, and I have
heard this more times than I can count. It is no secret that
people tend to procrastinate. They don't want to address
this subject even though they truly understand the need and
how the plan works. They just don't act. Procrastination is
the biggest killer of effective estate planning.

3. "I can get Mom to sign her name so we can go forward
with the documents."

This phrase addresses mental competency. A person may
not need to have the physical ability to sign documents as
long as the person understands the nature and extent of
what they are signing. Consider a quadriplegic who is per-
fectly competent. There is a legal process for that person to
sign documents even if he or she cannot move. On the other
hand, an incompetent person is legally incapable of signing
documents even if he or she is able to run a marathon.

4. "Medicare will pay for my mom's nursing home."

This is a fatal mistake in understanding. Medicare is a
health insurance program designed to pay for treatment
and care. It pays up to a maximum of one hundred days

in a nursing home, and only a portion of that cost after the first twenty of those hundred days. Typically, elders have a supplemental policy to cover the gap between Medicare and the nursing home cost. I have consistently told clients that Medicare will cover up to one hundred days, and they never believe me. So I generally have to work with the clients when they are in crisis, and unfortunately, many of their preferable planning options may no longer be available.

5. "My mom passed away, and the title insurance company will not honor my power of attorney."

All legal documents must be read in light of statutes and case law. In this case, the issue is very simple: all powers of attorney, no matter what the document states, terminate on the death of the creator of the power of attorney, whether the power of attorney states so or not.[4] Unfortunately, many people either read the document and generate their own conclusions or have talked to someone who obviously was not well versed in legal concepts.

6. "I have a financial power of attorney, but the stock company will not accept it."

I have found that this goes to the general lack of understanding of the complexities regarding financial powers of attorney. All powers of attorney are not the same! I outlined the issues with powers of attorney in chapter nine. Again, there are regular financial powers of attorney, special or limited financial powers of attorney, durable general or

---

4   In California, there are a few exceptions relating to burial.

limited financial powers of attorney, springing durable general or limited financial powers of attorney, and more. In addition, not all the powers of attorney authorize the same actions. As mentioned in chapter nine, in California, even general powers of attorney that state that the agent can do everything that the creator could do, by California law still lacks certain authority unless it is specifically stated in the document.

7. "I don't have enough money to need a living trust."

A common misconception is that the size of your estate determines whether or not you should consider a living trust. The type of asset and how it is held is what really matters. For example, when addressing probate avoidance, a person could own a small piece of real estate worth ten thousand dollars and the client lives in a trailer on the land. This would require a court petition in probate court to transfer the interest on death. However, another person could have a million dollars in certificates of deposit that are paid on death to specific people, and there may be no need for a living trust.[5] In both examples, however, if the owner of the assets was incompetent and did not have a living trust or other appropriate legal document, a court process would be required, such as a conservatorship or guardianship proceeding to transact business on behalf of the elder. Conservatorship and guardianship proceedings are expensive, stress-

---

5   There may be a variety of other reasons that this is not the best estate planning move and this needs to be discussed with legal counsel.

ful, and time-consuming court processes, and simple legal planning could avoid the problem if done ahead of time.

Whether a living trust would be beneficial is not as simple as it may seem. There are creditor claim issues, asset protection issues, and other legal issues that can affect the decision-making, in addition to the type of assets that the client has. The decision should be made together with the client's estate planning attorney.

8. "I can afford long-term care if I need it so I do not need to plan for this care."

This statement depends on the financial status of the client, but nursing home costs are through the roof and rising. If you are a wealthy individual with an estate greater than the fair market value of the nursing home itself, then you should just buy the nursing home so that your care can be provided to you. If not, I suspect that you will not be able to afford the monthly nursing home cost for any reasonable time.

In California, nursing homes average $7,628 per month (for 2014).[6] However, I have worked on cases where clients were institutionalized in subacute long-term care facilities (a type of nursing home) with costs exceeding $45,000 per month. This is unsustainable even if you are a multimillionaire.

9. "The clerk at the store said I don't need a living trust."

---

6   State of California Health and Human Services Agency (Department of Health Care Services), Medi-Cal General Property Limitations, Medi-Cal Information Notice 007, April 2014.

Yep! Believe it or not, I have heard this more times than I can count. I do not need to comment further.

10. "When my wife died, everything came to me. So why do I now need a living trust? It was so simple."

Often a husband and wife hold assets as joint tenants. By definition, joint tenancy states that when one of the two owners dies, that share by operation of law transfers to the survivor. There is little to do except take the decedent's name off of the account, which is usually done by simply providing a death certificate to the institution or bank.

However, when the second person dies, there is no longer a joint tenancy and thus the need for probate. Also, joint tenancy does not address incapacity of a joint owner. In fact, if a husband and wife owned a residence in joint tenancy and either become incompetent, the competent person cannot sell the home or refinance the home without a full conservatorship being obtained, unless there is a valid power of attorney with the appropriate authority to act.

11. "My husband took care of everything."

This one can almost stand without comment. Unfortunately, most people do not truly understand the nuances and complexity of estate planning. If it were simple, there would not be an entire industry, including lawyers, financial planners, accountants, and insurance professionals built around it. Having the belief that everything is taken care of without having consultation and preparation of the estate plan by a competent estate planning attorney is just burying one's head in the sand. It will cost money to do it right! However, this is the most important money that you will spend in your entire lifetime to ensure peace of mind that everything is properly prepared and addressed.

12. "My husband has all the information to take care of his mother."

I got into a discussion with a woman at a social event about preparation for an eldercare journey regarding her mother-in-law. She said she didn't need any help because her husband had everything prepared and arranged. I then asked what would happen if he were in an accident and died. Did she know what to do and whom to contact? Did she have any of the information discussed earlier in this book? Her face went white, and her jaw dropped!

13. "I don't need to pay an attorney that much. Don't you just put names into a computer and press the button?"

Most people look at living trusts and think they are all the same. This is very wrong. But more important, the documents are merely evidence of a legal service being provided. I tell my seminar attendees that I don't care if someone on death row types the documents as long they are the way that I want them to read. Drafting the document is quite different from determining *what* to draft!

Chapter 11

SAFETY CHECKLIST

THE TWO MOST COMMON CAUSES of trips to the hospital are falls and overmedication.

This book has given you the information that you will need on your eldercare journey. But, as they say, an ounce of prevention is worth a pound of cure. Taking reasonable steps to prevent a fall or an overdose (or under dose) can save a lot of anguish and possibly the elder's life.

The suggestions that follow may apply only to an elder living in his or her residence while others may apply in other living situations. This is intended to be an overview of issues that you should address.

Fall Risk Assessment

Regardless of where your elder lives, it behooves you to conduct your own fall risk assessment at the elder's residence. It may even help if you use a walker to mimic the actions and movements that the elder will take. I always wondered why on the police TV shows the detectives would walk through the crime at the crime scene. Being part of the crime scene engulfs the officers in the moment so that their minds are opened to the events. It is amazing what you miss by not putting yourself in the shoes of the elder and becoming the elder for the day.

Floors

In all areas of the living quarters, check for different floor levels. These are common where carpet connects with other types of flooring. Minimize large "lips" or thresholds between these levels. The entry into the residence can also have these. Doors to patios are notorious for having these lips as well. Find a way to perhaps bevel the lips up and down to smooth the path. Be creative.

In all areas of living quarters, check how slippery floor areas become if they are wet and take corrective action if it can cause a fall. Elders spill things, so the entire residence needs to be evaluated for slipping if it became wet. This is especially important for the shower and sink. All bathroom flooring should be a matte-finished type tile or low-pile carpet. Bathroom throw rugs are discouraged, but if the elder insists on a throw rug, it should have nonskid backing. You need to balance the fall risk of a wet floor with the fall risk of the elder getting his or her foot caught under the bath mat. Be sure that the shower or bathtub has nonskid mats. The kitchen is another high-moisture area that needs to be addressed if the flooring becomes wet.

Many people also find that grab-bars are helpful for elders with difficulty balancing. A grab-bar can sometimes prevent falls in showers or bathing areas, and it can even be helpful for elders who have already fallen, allowing them to get back up if they are physically able to do so. If possible, get rid of all throw rugs in the living areas.

Stairs

If there are stairs, check to see that the handrails are sturdy and reinforce them if necessary. Elders put a lot of pressure on handrails to keep balanced and to assist their legs in raising their bodies. Make sure that the steps are always clear of personal items. If the steps are not carpeted, perhaps use antiskid strips.

Cabinetry

Are the kitchen cabinets easily accessible? If they are too high, the elder can reach beyond where he or she should and lose balance. Similarly, are the cabinets too low, where if the elder leaned over, he or she could fall? Have the elder use only the cabinets that are easily accessible. Consider replacing shelving with pull-out drawers to avoid the elder leaning to grab items.

Are the bathroom cabinets also easily accessible? The cabinets under the bathroom sink pose a specific risk, as the floor might be wet when the elder is leaning over to reach items. Installing pull drawers here could offer added safety. Look at the entire environment and move around as though you were the elder. Make note of issues that need to be corrected.

Cords

I hate power cords, although we cannot live without them. Everything needs electricity or a connection to the outside world. However, these cords are like tripwires in the elder's home.

Elders still use corded phones, and all phones must be attached somewhere to the wall for electricity or access to the phone network. Notwithstanding where the elder would like to have the phone located, care must be taken to balance his or her wishes against safety hazards.

Similarly, electric cords for lamps, televisions, cable boxes, DVRs, CD players, and the senior's electric loungers must be addressed to remove these trip-wires from all the traffic areas. If necessary, you need to rearrange the living spaces to accommodate the fall risks. I remember my parents wanting the television on one side of the room, but the cable outlet was on the other side. They wanted to put a long cable cord against the wall all the way around to the other side. The cable cord would also lie right in front of the glass door slider to the patio. Ding, ding, ding: fall risk! We talked them into spending a little money and installing a cable outlet on the other side of the room.

Furniture

Check for furniture where the elder can get a foot caught and cause a fall. Even with her walker, my wife's mother caught her foot on a leg of her bed and went down. She broke her hip and spent eight weeks in a nursing home.

Is there furniture (such as chairs) with rollers that can slip away from the elder when he or she tries to sit? Is the furniture too low? Too high? Does the furniture have full and stable arms to assist the elder in lowering and rising up from the chair or couch? Is the seat too fluffy, where the elder can get "stuck" in the comfort of the chair? Is the chair stable enough? Pretend you are the elder and see what you think.

Walkers

Most elders will at some point need to use a walker. Can the walker cleanly fit through all areas of the residence without having to turn it sideways or without requiring the elder to leave the walker behind for the moment, including in the bathroom?

Is the walker steady? In good state of repair?

If your elder is not yet using a walker, do his or her shoes give the needed support? Can the elder easily put on their shoes without bending over too far?

Look for areas that require the elder to lean down to avoid items, such as lamps or other hangings. I have seen this often where the lamp next to the recliner causes the elder to lean to the side to sit down. This can cause him or her to lose balance.

Lighting

This is very important. I suggest that you have nightlights throughout the residence. If night lights are turned on in each room, do they adequately cover all travel areas? If there are stairs, consider small floor lights on the stairs so that they can clearly be seen.

Is there adequate lighting in the kitchen for cooking and moving about?

Perhaps use lighted light switches throughout the residence so the elder can clearly see where to turn on lights.

Miscellaneous

The bathroom is a high-risk fall area because the elder needs to move—turning around, sitting and standing up from the toilet, and stepping in and out of bathing areas—in a very small area. This activity is usually without the aid of the walker. The bathroom should be equipped with grab-bars in the shower and by the toilet. The more bars, the merrier.

The showerhead should be within easy reach. Soap and shampoo products need to be easily handled and at a convenient height. The towel bar needs to be easily accessible.

Our parents have had to move multiple times and I expect a couple more moves. Through my experiences, I created a comprehensive fall-safety checklist that is included in my *ElderCare Ready Pack*, which is available by going to my website at www.eldercareready.com

Medicine management

Medicine management is critical to your elder's well-being. If the medicines are managed by the community or facility where he or she lives, your elder is much safer from the risk of overdosing. This system is not perfect as the medicine staff person can also make mistakes, so it is important to check with them periodically. If the elder does not have this type of service, you need to assist the elder with preparing the medicine containers (also called "pillboxes," which are containers that have the day and week pill compartments) and monitor and confirm that the elder takes only the appropriate pill allocation. Elders often forget which day it is or what they have already taken that day. They can panic and take a double dose from another day's container of pills. This "med management" is perhaps the most important item discussed in this book as the drugs are often the most deadly. By the way, if they overdose (or under dose) and go to the hospital, your medication list will be invaluable and help save your elder's life. As I said, a crisis can occur at any time without notice. Be prepared!

Chapter 12

SECURITY CHECK

WHETHER LIVING AT HOME OR in a facility, theft is on the rise. I have to admit that my mother-in-law was a victim of theft in two different assisted living communities. Don't expect the facility to take responsibility for the loss because the facilities say it is up to the resident to protect his or her valuables. I have heard facilities promote their communities as safe and secure places for your elder to live, but on the other hand, they say that theft is rampant, is part of the assisted living experience, and that each resident needs to protect his or her own property.

Always remove valuables from your loved one when he or she is in the hospital or nursing home. These are usually temporary stays, and elders do not need to look good. They are there to get healthy.

In board and care, there is also very little need for many valuables. Most often, the women like to wear their wedding rings. But be cautious because as they lose weight, their fingers also lose size, and the ring can easily fall off and get lost. There is a tendency to accuse someone of stealing, but most often, this is not the case.

In assisted living or independent living communities, many people have access to your elder's room, including the cleaning staff, the medicine management staff, the executive director staff, and others. My mother-in-law had all her jewelry stolen by a person who was prosecuted, but the case was dismissed on a technicality. The jewelry dating back to her grandmother was gone forever. My mother-in-law was heartbroken, but there was nothing we could do. Always carry renter's insurance to cover the financial loss, even though it cannot replace the emotional loss.

If requested, most assisted and independent living communities will provide a locked closet door to protect the elder's valuables.

If the elder lives at home, a homeowner's policy usually covers losses; even so, protect your elder's stuff as well as you can, as the emotional damage due to a loss cannot be fixed.

Chapter 13

WHAT TO EXPECT FROM CARE PROVIDERS

Pickles by Brian Crane

WHAT'S THE MATTER, EARL? YOU LOOK A LITTLE DOWN.

ACCORDING TO STATISTICS, I HAVE A BETTER THAN FIFTY PERCENT CHANCE OF LIVING TO THE AGE OF EIGHTY-SEVEN.

9/8

WHAT'S WRONG WITH THAT?

I CAN'T AFFORD TO LIVE THAT LONG.

THE FOLLOWING ARE VERY GENERAL definitions of different types of care and facilities that you will need to understand. Please be aware that in states other than California, these terms and the licensing (affecting the type of resident that may be admitted) for each level may be different. But this should provide a general understanding of care options for each level of care.

Home Care

Home care is provided in a person's home and is designed to provide support for those who are still able to live at home. This type of care is traditionally provided by licensed professionals in the case of medical care or by nonlicensed professionals for nonmedical care (such as helping with daily living activities).

Home care is a variable term that can cover several different types of care. Nonmedical services can include assistance with daily tasks, such as meal preparation, shopping, errands, light housekeeping, transportation, laundry, and companionship. Medical services provided in the home sometimes differentiate themselves from these nonmedical service providers by the use of the term home health care.

Home health care covers specifically licensed care providers who administer medical services at a patient's home, often because of illness, injury, or sudden health difficulties. Services can include some of the following duties:

- Wound care for pressure (bed) sores or surgical wounds
- Patient and caregiver education
- Injections
- Monitoring serious illnesses
- Nutrition therapy (including intravenous therapy)
- Taking blood and monitoring blood chemistry and other vital measurements

Home health care is designed to help patients to recover from serious injury or illness so those persons can regain independence and become self-sufficient again.

Assisted Living and Independent Living

Assisted living and independent living are designed for more able individuals and are usually provided in large community buildings with perhaps tens or hundreds of apartment-like units. Some facilities even offer individual, private, freestanding home units for residents. These spaces may come furnished or unfurnished, and most include a bedroom, kitchen area, and bathroom. These facilities are usually offered as studio apartments, one-bedroom apartments, or two-bedroom apartments.

The cost of living at these communities can vary widely. In addition, some facilities operate on a long-term contract basis (often called a buy-in program) with up-front costs, and others operate on shorter term or month-to-month contracts with residents.

The services offered may include the following:

- Housekeeping and maintenance

- Organized recreational activities

- Laundry services

- Assistance with daily living activities (bathing, dressing, eating, toileting, etc.)

- Medication management

- Central dining programs that include two or three meals a day

- Educational activities

- Exercise activities

- Emergency call systems in private and common areas

- Social services and religious activities

- Transportation arrangements

- Wellness programs

- Twenty-four hour security

Pricing for these living arrangements is determined based on the size of the unit as well as the care services offered. Most facilities allow residents to choose services based on their levels of need.

Memory Care

Older persons suffering from Alzheimer's disease, dementia, or other illness affecting their memory and awareness often need to live in a secure environment to prevent wandering. Most people who suffer from these diseases will eventually require twenty-four hour supervision. Memory care facilities are designed to provide care to these types of patients.

Some memory care facilities are housed inside larger assisted living facilities, and some are standalone facilities that cater only to memory care residents. These facilities, whether part of a larger facility or standing on their own, provide long-term care to seniors with memory issues. The ratio of caregivers to patients is usually higher than in a regular assisted living facility, and the level of care offered is often more comprehensive as well. Staff members typically have greater training requirements when compared to traditional assisted living facilities due to the higher health demands of the residents. Costs may vary, with some facilities charging fees on par with assisted living facilities, while others charge a comparatively higher amount due to the added supervision and services provided.

As with assisted living facilities, rooms may be private or semiprivate, and living spaces may come furnished or unfurnished, depending on the facility. The size of the living space will also help to determine the cost of the residence.

In addition to the increased supervision and secure facility features, the services that are offered may include the following:

- Housekeeping and maintenance
- Organized recreational activities
- Laundry services
- Assistance with daily living activities (bathing, dressing, eating, toileting, etc.)
- Medication management

- Central dining programs that include two or three meals a day
- Educational activities
- Exercise activities
- Emergency call systems in private and common areas
- Social services and religious activities
- Transportation arrangements
- Wellness programs
- Twenty-four hour security

Board and Care (Residential Care Facility for the Elderly)

A board and care home is usually a six-bed home and is typically in a residential community. These are typically for more acute-care individuals who do not need skilled care. All services for activities of daily living (bathing, toileting, feeding, grooming, etc.) are provided as needed. All meals are provided. Some homes have hospice waivers, allowing them to care for and house hospice patients, and some may also take nonambulatory residents, but this varies from home to home.

Skilled Nursing (Nursing Home)

Skilled nursing facilities, often called "nursing homes," provide skilled (medically trained) care to residents 24/7. These trained professionals usually perform services on a temporary rather than a long-term basis for people who have experienced an injury or illness. The following are some example situations where a person might need skilled nursing services:

- A licensed nurse in a skilled nursing facility providing postoperative wound care and monitoring medications for a skilled nursing resident who has recently been released from the hospital following a surgical procedure
- An occupational therapist helping a resident to become independent and self-sufficient during a stay in a skilled nursing facility (assisting with therapy to help the person with dressing, personal hygiene, and eating)
- A physical therapist helping a resident become mobile again by overcoming issues with strength and balance
- A speech therapist helping a skilled nursing facility resident to communicate again following a stroke that affected their ability to communicate

Varying degrees of care may be provided at a skilled nursing facility. Some services are provided on a temporary basis and are designed to restore a resident's ability to live independently. These rehabilitative services may include assistance and therapy for some of the following items:

- Bathing
- Dressing
- Personal hygiene
- Eating
- Maneuvering in and out of bed/walking
- Incontinence
- Other activities of daily living

Skilled nursing facilities can also be divided between facilities that provide what is called subacute care and those that provide traditional levels of care as discussed in this section. Subacute facilities are a provider between a full hospital and a standard skilled nursing facility. These more advanced facilities are able to provide more sophisticated or complex medical support to patients who are experiencing more severe injuries or illnesses. Subacute care facilities may provide care for needs such as the following:

- Complex wound care
- Feeding tube therapy
- Ventilation (assistance with breathing)
- Postsurgical care
- Dialysis

Most traditional skilled nursing facilities also provide care for persons who are suffering from more serious or terminal diseases or ailments. In some cases, a person may reside in a skilled nursing facility or nursing home permanently, especially in situations where he or she has an illness that necessitates skilled care and where rehabilitation is not an option.

Together with the services discussed above, a skilled nursing facility or nursing home may also provide the following:

- Limited transportation services
- Laundry services
- Social and educational activities
- Pharmaceutical, radiology, and/or laboratory services

- End-of-life/hospice care
- Respite care

Rehabilitation Facilities

A rehabilitation facility or inpatient rehabilitation facility is for patients undergoing treatment following a stay in the hospital. The goal of a rehabilitation center is to help a person to regain independence following an illness or injury. Unlike a skilled nursing facility or nursing home, a rehabilitation facility is not designed for long-term care but for a shorter term stay aimed at returning the patient home as soon as possible. If a person is not able to become independent within a short time, a decision may be made to move that person to a skilled nursing facility for more long-term care.

Rehabilitation facilities promote the independence of the patient by offering therapy to residents. Common rehabilitative services offered at these facilities may include the following:

- Occupational therapy
- Speech therapy
- Physical therapy
- Counseling
- Nutritional therapy and counseling

Note on Care Homes: Many of the above care home types combine various levels of care or service in one facility (such as a large assisted living community also having a memory care section), so there is often no clear line where one type of facility may no longer be appropriate and another might be needed.

Hospice

Hospice care is given to patients who are facing terminal illnesses or who are near death. A person is usually placed on hospice care once it has been determined that illness or injury is not likely to improve and will result in death within a foreseeable length of time (usually six months). After hospice treatment begins, all therapies and treatments (including medication) designed to combat the illness are stopped and only medicine and other treatments designed to make the person comfortable and to alleviate pain are administered. Hospice care can make a person's last days, weeks, or even months more bearable and improve quality of life. Hospice care can be provided in a person's home or in a medical facility (such as assisted living, memory care, or a nursing home).

Typical Cost of Care[7]

The cost of care can vary widely depending on the geographical region where the care or resident is located, the services provided, and the size and level of comfort of the accommodation at hand. Typical costs given here are estimates based on the average costs (nationwide) for each type of care, so it is important to remember that an individual

---

7   Cost Data Source: Genworth Financial, Inc. Executive Summary: Genworth 2014 Cost of Care Survey. 2014. https://www.genworth.com/dam/Americas/US/PDFs/Consumer/corporate/131168-032514-Executive-Summary-nonsecure.pdf

may experience a cost of care that can fall far outside of the ranges below, particularly in areas of the country that have a higher than average cost of living or cost of medical care (such as California, New York, New Jersey, and Alaska).

Home Care

Home-care providers most often charge hourly rates for their services. Less skilled service providers (nonmedical) who help with activities such as housekeeping, errands, and meal preparation generally charge an average of $19.00 per hour, nationwide. Home health aides (medical service providers) tend to charge a higher average rate of $20.00 per hour, nationwide. These hourly rates will vary depending on the state in which the service is being performed, often due to local and state labor laws regarding wage and hour treatment for home-care providers.

Assisted Living

The national average (median) for a one-bedroom unit in an assisted living facility in 2014 was approximately $3,500 per month. Many facilities charge additional fees if there is another resident (such as a spouse) in addition to the base charge for the first resident. Facilities may also charge one-time fees upon entrance into the facility. Care services usually come at an additional charge on top of the rent paid per month, often on a package or calculated basis, depending on the services provided. While there are sometimes public benefits available to help seniors afford this type of residence, Medicare and state insurance programs generally do not provide assistance with paying for assisted living costs.

Memory Care

The type and availability of memory care facilities tends to vary more widely than at assisted living facilities, making it more difficult to estimate an average cost of care nationwide. Due to the additional services and security provided at memory care facilities, average annual costs tend to be higher than those at assisted living facilities, coming in at around $5,000 per month (for a single resident in a single bedroom accommodation) nationwide. As with assisted living costs, additional services and accommodation options will add to the monthly cost. As with assisted living facilities, Medicare and state insurance programs will not usually help offset the cost of memory care accommodation.

Board and Care (Residential Care Facility for the Elderly)

Most board-and-care homes are smaller operations, which results in monthly costs that typically fall between the range of assisted living and memory care facilities. These smaller, more personalized homes provide a higher degree of care (in general) than assisted living facilities offer, but the cost is usually only marginally higher. Costs will vary depending on the region in which the facility is situated and the level of care that the patient or resident requires.

Skilled Nursing Facilities

Skilled nursing facility charges are most often measured with a daily rate because a patient's term of stay can vary widely depending on the level of care needed and the illness or injury being treated. The national average per day for a private room in a skilled nursing facility is $240 per day, while the average for a shared or semiprivate room is $212 per day. These rates are most often all-inclusive, meaning that the daily rate usually includes all services available to the resident, rather than a calculated charge based on the particular care services being used by the resident. In cases where a senior has spent three midnights in a hospital after being admitted, Medicare will often pay for a portion of a resident's stay, and after that coverage period has elapsed, a resident is expected to provide for the cost of their own care. Sometimes, private health insurance will also cover a portion of a policyholder's stay in a skilled nursing facility as well.

Rehabilitation Facilities

It is difficult to estimate the average cost of rehabilitation facilities, given that in most cases, a person's stay in a rehabilitation facility is usually covered by Medicare or private insurance. In the event that a person is required to pay for rehabilitation, costs will vary depending on the services provided and the region in which the elder resides.

Hospice

A person's hospice-related care is usually covered by Medicare. In the event that a person is required to pay for hospice (which is rare), costs will vary depending on the services provided and the region in which the elder resides.

Chapter 14

WHAT TO DO AFTER THE DEATH OF A LOVED ONE

Pickles by Brian Crane

OPAL, WOULD YOU SAY WE'RE HAPPY?

OF COURSE WE'RE HAPPY.

I MEAN, SOMETIMES YOU CAN GO THROUGH LIFE NOT REALLY KNOWING IF YOU'RE HAPPY OR NOT.

AND IT'S NOT UNTIL YOU LOOK BACK ON IT YEARS LATER THAT YOU REALIZE YOU ACTUALLY WERE HAPPY.

TAKE MY WORD FOR IT, YOU'RE EXTREMELY HAPPY.

THAT'S GOOD TO KNOW.

SINCE MANY ACTIONS CAN AFFECT the deceased elder's estate, including but not limited to, tax and other elections that may be beneficial in the administration of an estate, I suggest that, after a loved one's passing, no action other than the below be taken without the advice and counsel of an estate planning attorney.

As Soon as Possible

1. Determine whether any of decedent's property needs to be safeguarded, such as a motor vehicle, vacant residence or rental house, and the like. Secure property from potential loss such as theft and vandalism.

2. Ensure that proper funeral arrangements have been made and carried out per the wishes of the elder. The funeral home should order death certificates, and normally six to twelve of them are sufficient. For larger estates, one certificate per deed or financial account may be needed.

3. Contact an estate planning attorney such as myself immediately and engage the firm for legal services relating to settlement and administration of the trust and/or estate. If the elder does not have an estate planning attorney, please feel free to contact my office for a possible referral. I can

be reached by email at sfurman@socallegalcenter.com or by phone (toll free) at (877) 820-3335.

4. Take possession of the original living trust and last will documents. Do not write on original documents.

5. Meet with the attorney and follow his/her instructions.

6. Bring your *ElderCare Ready Book* or *ElderCare Ready Pack* information and documentation to the consultation. The attorney will be very impressed, and it will save you attorney's fees!

Chapter 15

EPILOGUE

AFTER FINISHING THIS BOOK, MY father died on October 18, 2014, completing his life journey. Our final elder-care excursion with him began in the morning of October 17, 2014, when we were called by the owner of the board and care home where he resided. She said that in the middle of the night he had aspirated and it appeared that he had another reoccurring infection. She felt it necessary to dial 911 and take him to the emergency room.

We were all well acquainted with the ER as we have been there often with all three of our parents, from time to time. We called the hospital our "condo" or "time share" as we were there so often.

My dad was unconscious and hooked up to IVs when my wife and I arrived. There were several nurses and doctors that came in and out, testing him to get a diagnosis. The doctor informed us that dad had sepsis and his prognosis was not good. The rest of the family was summoned to the hospital in case the worst happened.

There was ultimately a choice that had to be made: whether to provide additional treatment or to let him pass peacefully. This is the type of decision that every child hopes that they never have to make. But the options were presented nonetheless, and a choice had to be made.

Option one was to give him a central line which would quickly pump large doses of antibiotics into his system in hopes of stemming his infection. This had to be done in an ICU unit and under very sterile conditions. It was somewhat invasive. With this he had a "Hail Mary" chance of surviving the infection.

Option two was to step back, rather than make any invasive procedures, and prepare for his passing in a hospital room with his family at his bedside.

There were discussions as to whether the central line was "heroic" in nature. Interestingly each of the two doctors had differing opinions. So the choice was down to the family decision.

Ultimately we all decided it was best for no treatment to be provided. If the central line was effective, what was his quality of life going to be? The doctors said that he would not even come back to the original baseline condition and that his current condition was already dire. The doctors also said that even with the central line, in their opinion the outcome would be the same.

Dad was moved to a regular room in the hospital and we waited. The hospital staff was incredibly compassionate. This had to be difficult for them as well as they are healers and it is difficult to see their patients die.

All of our eyes were glued to the monitors for some reason. We all knew what was coming, but perhaps it was the weird intrigue with the dying process. At 1:41 the next morning my dad slipped away and died peacefully in his sleep. His long and difficult journey was over and he was at peace.

Our eldercare journey however was not yet over. Immediately after his passing I was approached by the hospital staff about donating his eyes to research. He had glaucoma and they wanted his eyes for medical research. We all agreed and it was done. Being prepared for this postmortem work should not be overlooked. While dealing with the loss of your loved one, there are important decisions that still need to be made.

Dad was cremated and prepared for scattering his ashes at sea. We had a truly great celebration of life party that we named a "roast and toast" to tell funny stories and serious ones. Guests were in tears but we enjoyed the reminiscing.

That was how his incredible life ended. He now lives on in our memories...

Chapter 16

GLOSSARY OF TERMS AND EXPLANATIONS

assessor's parcel number. The descriptive number assigned to real estate for tax assessment tracking purposes.

beneficiary. The person or organization entitled to the benefits of an estate, trust, life insurance policy, IRA, or other asset.

deferred annuity. An annuity contract where the funds compound tax deferred (meaning income tax is not paid on the earnings until they are withdrawn). These annuities are typically revocable and subject to paying a surrender charge for an early withdrawal. Surrender charges expire after a certain period as determined by the annuity contract.

estate planning. The planning for the transfer of assets upon death or for change in control if one is incapacitated.

health care advance directive. These are known by various other names across the country, including being called a "medical power of attorney." These documents grant the authority to another person to make medical decisions for you if you are unable to do so for yourself (due to legal incompetency or being sedated during surgery, etc.).

HIPAA release. A HIPAA release is similar to a general consent to release your medical information to the persons named in the HIPAA release.

hospice. A program paid through Medicare designed to assist people in the process of dying. All medicines designed to treat a person's illness are halted and only comfort medicines are provided to relieve pain. Hospice generally also provides counseling.

immediate annuity. An irrevocable annuity that pays a monthly amount to the annuitant (the person whose life the annuity is based upon) until the selected term expires or the annuitant dies.

impound account. Sometimes a lender on a home mortgage collects additional funds within the mortgage payment to pay the real estate taxes and insurance premiums and pays them when due. This account where that money is held is called an impound account.

irrevocable trust. A living trust that cannot be revoked, amended, or modified by the creator once signed.

living trust. An estate planning document executed to generally avoid probate and conservatorship (sometimes called guardianship for adults) proceedings. Assets are transferred to the named trustee, typically the creator of the trust, to be managed according to the trust provisions. In the event of the death or incapacity of the creator of the trust, the successor trustee takes over allowing for the smooth management transition.

long-term care insurance (LTCI). Insurance that provides benefits for stays in nursing homes, assisted living, and sometimes in independent living communities. The LTCI policy may also provide benefits for care at home. All policies are different. This is not a government program and is privately purchased.

Medicaid (Medi-Cal in California). A federal program implemented through the states; however, each state can and often does vary considerably on the implementation. California refers to its Medicaid program as Medi-Cal. Your state may also refer to Medicaid by a more generic name. The program provides financial support for long-term care in a nursing facility. Some states have programs to provide Medicaid benefits at the board-and-care level, and some programs provide benefits for care at home.

Medicare. The health insurance program for individuals available to those over the age of sixty-five. There are other health insurance programs under Medicare for disabled and other individuals that are not referred to in this book.

nonrecurring medications. Medications taken for a specific illness or issue and intended to be stopped once the illness is cured.

nonqualified accounts. Accounts that are not qualified accounts. These are also referred to as nonretirement accounts. See "qualified accounts" on the following page.

pour-over will. A will that names the creator's living trust as the beneficiary.

power of attorney. A document authorizing a person to act on behalf of another according to the terms of the document.

current durable power of attorney. A durable power of attorney that stays in effect after the principal (the one granting the power of attorney) has become legally incompetent.

springing durable power of attorney. A durable power of attorney that becomes effective ONLY after the principal (the one granting the power of attorney) has become legally incompetent. It "springs" into effect upon incapacity or when another condition is fulfilled which triggers the authority coming into effect. The threshold must be satisfied before the agent can use the power of attorney.

qualified account. A specific tax-deferred retirement account where no income taxes are paid on the income until it is withdrawn. The most common qualified accounts are IRAs and a 401(k). These are also referred to as retirement accounts.

recurring medications. Medications taken at prescribed intervals that are intended to continue indefinitely.

release on file. Please see detailed information on releases in chapter 9.

revocable trust. A living trust that can be revoked, amended, or modified by the creator.

RN or LVN. An RN is a registered nurse while an LVN is a licensed vocational nurse.

Rx name. The name of the medication.

settlor. The settlor is the creator of a living trust. The settlor may also be referred to as the trustor, grantor, transferor, creator, or trustmaker.

successor trustee. The individual or institution managing the trust if the initial trustee has died or is incapacitated.

skilled nursing home. Commonly known as a nursing home or convalescent home. Rehabilitation facilities sometimes come under this name.

testamentary trust. A trust created within a last will and testament.

trustee. The individual or institution who manages a trust.

veterans' benefits. A generic term to mean a pension paid to veterans meeting certain tests, and to their surviving spouses, to pay for costs of long-term care in an assisted living facility, board-and-care home, and for care at home. This is not referring to disability or compensation payments due to a service connected injury.

vesting. This is another word for whose name an asset is in. An account is "vested" in your name if your name appears on the account as opposed to an account that is in your living trust, in which case the account is vested in your living trust.

THE ELDERCARE
READY SYSTEM

THE THEME THROUGHOUT THIS BOOK has been to prepare for your eldercare journey, not to fear it. You will need to take this journey at some point, so make your travel plans now before the crisis hits.

You will need a lot of information and documentation for your eldercare journey, and it is very difficult to organize it in an efficient manner. I worked countless hours creating an organized handbook to assist me and have made this manual available to my readers.

The ElderCare Ready Pack is a powerful system to manage your elder's medical, financial, emotional, and logistical affairs.

If you want to simplify your life and not reinvent the wheel, please visit my website at **www.eldercareready.com** to acquire one of these truly unique handbooks. The *ElderCare Ready Pack* contains over a hundred pages of detailed outlines prompting you for exactly the information and documentation that you will need. The fill-in-the–blanks format will ensure that you don't miss important information along your journey.

Be sure to also visit my website at www.eldercareready.com for:

- Updates to documentation and information that you may need
- Updates on legal and financial issues affecting your eldercare journey
- Current news affecting eldercare
- Helpful tips and great ideas submitted to me from my readers
- Funny stories and elder jokes
- Other stories and personal thoughts of mine and those of my readers
- Valuable resources to assist you in specific areas

You can also contact me about ElderCare Ready at:

Stuart Furman, Esq.
sfurman@eldercareready.com
1-800-551-7505

About the Author

STUART FURMAN, ESQ.

STUART FURMAN HAS BEEN A member of the State Bar for the state of California and has been practicing law since 1981. He was accredited by the Department of Veterans Affairs as an accredited VA attorney in 2009. Mr. Furman's law practice has concentrated on elder law issues, including long-term care for seniors, planning for veterans and accessing VA benefits, Medi-Cal/Medicaid pre-planning and accessing Medi-Cal and Medicaid benefits, living trusts, wills, powers of attorney, advanced medical directives, and other peripheral issues.

Mr. Furman has educated nurses, discharge planners, and social workers in many Southern California hospitals. He has appeared as a guest on several radio programs in Southern California. Mr. Furman has spoken for numerous organizations around California and has offered continuing education credits for real estate agents and brokers, board-and-care administrators, CPAs, EAs, and other professionals.

Mr. Furman is vice chair and sits on the board of directors of a large Visiting Nurses Association and hospice organization in Southern California. He is a member of the National Association of Elder Law Attorneys, ElderCounsel, the San

Diego Society of Human Resource Management (SDSHRM), and is on the legislative committee for SDSHRM.

In his personal life, he has enjoyed his marriage to his wife Jayne for more than twenty-three years. He is an accomplished violinist, having begun the study of music at the age of nine. He has sat on the board of directors of several musical organizations and performed as a member of several professional orchestras across the United States.

Mr. Furman is available to speak about planning for eldercare, eldercare legal issues, long-term care planning, and general eldercare topics at your company HR department and to your employees, community center, assisted living community, radio or television program, or other appropriate venues or events.

Stuart Furman is also the owner of Southern California Legal Center, Inc. where he practices elder law with clients located throughout California. His law practice can be reached at (877) 820-3335 or by email at:

sfurman@socallegalcenter.com

CPSIA information can be obtained
at www.ICGtesting.com
Printed in the USA
LVHW032130120721
692483LV00004B/744